THE PREACHER

MY LIFE, MY HEART, MY SHIVA

ROHIT PEGU

Made with ♥ on the Notion Press Platform
www.notionpress.com

To Lord Shiva, Sri Sri Thakur Anukulchandra and My Loving Parents

- Dedicated the book to Lord Shiva, Anukul Thakur, and my parents who gave me a beautiful life.
- Adding a final chapter with a heartfelt message for readers who may still be lost, urging them to find light through devotion and surrender
- Including some powerful mantras and prayers like the MahamrityunjayaMantra and Karpur Gauram Karunavtaram to deepen the spiritual connection for readers.

I can feel the purity of my heart, and this book will become a **DIVINE** offering to Lord Shiva, Anukul Thakur and my loving parents who gave me a beautiful life with love and care.

I will now begin working on the full spiritual book, ensuring it carries:

- My powerful life story — my loneliness, struggles, my turn to liquor, and my eventual salvation through Lord Shiva.
- Heartfelt prayers and chants like **Om Namah Shivay, Radha Swami,** and invocations to **Anukul Thakur.**
- A strong and moving dedication page that will honor all three — Lord Shiva, **Anukul Thakur,** and my parents.
- A powerful closing message encouraging others to find peace through devotion and surrender.

1. I am writing the book as if I am narrating it directly.
2. I have included visions, spiritual experiences or moments of **DIVINE** grace I felt when connecting with Lord Shiva.
3. Adding a special prayer section in the end that readers can chant daily for healing and guidance.

Contents

Preface

A Journey of Light and Devotion
Om Namah Shivaya Radha Swami
(Chant each three times for enlightenment)

There comes a moment in life when the soul yearns for something beyond the material world. A longing that no success, no relationship, and no earthly pleasure can fulfill. It is the call of the **DIVINE**—a whisper from within, urging us to seek truth, peace, and eternal love.

My journey has been one of solitude, introspection, and deep transformation. I have walked the path of a loner, searching for meaning in a world that often felt unfamiliar. But in my moments of darkness, I found light—through the blessings of **Sri Sri Thakur Anukulchandra** and the infinite grace of **Lord Shiva**. Their presence in my life has been my anchor, my guide, and my ultimate source of healing.

Born into an uncertain beginning, I was given the gift of loving parents who provided me with a life of abundance, values, and spiritual wisdom. From childhood, I was introduced to **Sri Sri Thakur Anukulchandra** teachings, which shaped my life's direction. But it was during a time of great turmoil that I truly turned to **Lord Shiva**, chanting his name, surrendering my worries, and embracing his boundless energy. From that moment, he has never left my side.

Every evening, as I sit with my mother for **Binati Prarthana**, I feel the divine presence of **Sri Sri Anukulchandra Thakur, Boroma, Borda** and **Ashokda** guiding me. In those sacred moments, my mind forgets all burdens and slips into deep meditation, where peace and divine love embrace me. No matter how weary the day has left me, prayer restores my soul.

This book is not just a collection of words; it is my offering to the **DIVINE**. It is a humble attempt to share the path that has transformed my life and to remind you that faith must come from the heart—it cannot be followed blindly. I hope these pages bring you closer to your own spiritual awakening and help you discover the immeasurable power of devotion, prayer, and inner surrender.

May the sacred chants of "Om **Namah Shivaya"** and the wisdom of the Gurus **"Guru mantra"** illuminate your journey as they have illuminated mine.

'Om Namah Shivaya'
'Om Namah Shivaya'
'Om Namah Shivaya'

'Radha Swami'
'Radha Swami'
'Radha Swami'

Sacred Beginnings: My Journey To Spirituality

My Story – How My Life Led Me to Spirituality and Devotion

Life has a way of leading us down unexpected paths, and my journey has been no exception. Though my adoptive parents provided me with a loving and nurturing home, there were times when I felt lost, searching for something beyond material success and worldly comforts. I faced struggles that tested my spirit, moments of doubt that left me yearning for deeper meaning. Yet, in those very moments, I found the whispers of divine intervention—guiding me, healing me, and showing me the way forward.

Through experiences of hardship and transformation, I discovered that spirituality is not just about rituals or traditions but about an intimate connection with the **DIVINE**. My journey was one of seeking, questioning, and ultimately finding peace in devotion. The turning points in my life were not just obstacles but stepping stones toward a higher understanding of myself and the universe.

The Purpose of This Book – Why I Am Sharing This Journey and How It Can Help Others

I write this book not just to recount my personal experiences but to offer a guiding light for those who may be searching for clarity, peace, or a deeper spiritual connection. Perhaps you, dear reader, have felt lost at times, longing for something more. My hope is that by sharing my story—the blessings I have received, the wisdom I have gained—you, too, may find comfort and direction in your own spiritual path.

Spirituality is not confined to grand acts or profound revelations; it is woven into the fabric of daily life. It is in the small moments of awareness, in the quiet surrender to faith, and in the courage to trust in something greater than ourselves. This book is an offering of love and insight, meant to remind you that no one walks alone on this journey

Sacred Invocation – Beginning with a Chant, Such as 'Om Namah Shivaya' or 'Radha Swami,' to Bless the Journey Ahead

Before we begin this journey, I invite you to take a deep breath and center yourself in the present moment. While this book unfolds my personal path, it is also an opportunity for you to reflect on your own spiritual experiences. Whether through prayer, meditation, or silent contemplation, each of us finds our own way to connect with the **DIVINE**.

Rather than opening with a specific chant or mantra, I encourage you, dear reader, to embrace whatever sacred practice resonates with your soul. Spirituality is deeply personal, and the vibrations of devotion are not limited to any one form. As you move through these pages, may you find inspiration to cultivate your own connection with the **DIVINE** in a way that is heartfelt and meaningful to you.

THE PREACHER

CHAPTER ONE

I wandered aimlessly, searching for enlightenment in a world that felt shrouded in uncertainty. Every path I took led to more questions—each one heavier than the last, pressing against my weary soul. It wasn't darkness that clouded this world, but a profound emptiness—a silence that echoed through the **hearts** of those who longed for something beyond the ordinary.

Days blurred into nights, and the nights stretched into an abyss of restless thoughts. I prayed, yet the heavens remained still. I cried out, but my voice dissolved into the vast emptiness. I sought answers, only to watch them slip away like whispers in the wind. This world—so unfamiliar, so unforeseen—was not one I had braced myself for. And yet, as I walked on, my soul, aching and parched, found solace in a quiet, unshaken chant...

> **"Om Namah Shivay... Om Namah Shivay...**
> **Om Namah Shivay..."**

I did not understand why I said it, but the vibration of those words brought a shiver to my spine. I felt something shifted within me — as if the darkness began to tremble. I kept walking and chanting, my voice cracking but my spirit awakening. And then, like a flicker of light in the depths of a long and dark tunnel, as if led by an unseen force, I stumbled upon a place I never imagined would hold significance for my wandering heart American Heart Association.

At first, it seemed absurd. Why would a seeker of truth and wisdom find himself standing before the doors of an institution dedicated to the physical **heart**? What connection did my spiritual longing have with their mission of healing flesh and blood? But something within me — a force I could not name, urged me to enter. "Why am I here?" I wondered. "What does the **heart** have to do with my quest for enlightenment?" But something within me urged me to step inside. I obeyed.

Inside, the air was heavy with stories of survival, loss, and miraculous resurrections. Photographs of people who had touched the threshold of death and returned, now smiled from the walls. Medical diagrams, **heart** monitors, and scientific jargon filled the space, but underneath it all, there was something deeper — something that my soul recognized immediately. I sat in a corner, my **heart** pounding. The realization was slow, but it came like tidal wave -**THE HEART**.

The **heart** is not merely an organ; it is the **temple of life**. It is the place where the **divine** resides. I had been searching for enlightenment in the vast cosmos when the greatest temple was within me within my **heart**, beating without pause. I closed my eyes and began to chant again — louder, deeper, more intentional...

"Om Namah Shivay...Om Namah Shivay...
Om Namah Shivay..."

It was **LIFE**. These people were not merely treating **hearts**; they were saving lives. They were restoring hope to families, reuniting children with their parents, and defying the cold grasp of death. Without knowing it, they were **preachers** of a different kind. Their sermons were written not in ink but in acts of love. Their message was not delivered from a pulpit but through the healing touch of their hands.

I sat quietly in a corner, watching them, listening to the rhythm of heart monitors and the hum of **life** around me. It was there, in that unexpected place, that I found a profound truth — the heart is not merely an organ; it is a symbol of existence, of love, of life itself.
And then it struck me — **I, too, is a Preacher.**

I had spent my days searching for divine enlightenment, not realizing that the greatest message was already beating within my chest. The darkness of the world was not the absence of **DIVINE** light but the absence of love — and love begins at **THE HEART**.

So, I rose, no longer searching, but now knowing. My mission was clear. If I could inspire love, if I could heal **hearts** — spiritually, emotionally or even metaphorically — then I would fulfill the calling that I had long misunderstood.

I walked out of the **American Heart Association** not as a lost soul but as a **Preacher of Love** — a preacher who now understood that the greatest gospel is life itself, and the purest sermon is the heartbeat of humanity. I added more spirituality by chanting 3 times chanting for each to get enlightened.

'Om Namah Shivaya'
'Om Namah Shivaya'
'Om Namah Shivaya'
'Radha Swami'
'Radha Swami'
'Radha Swami'

I have infused deep spiritual undertones, invoking the essence of **DIVINE** chants and the search for enlightenment.

CHAPTER TWO

The Preacher second stage

I had often heard stories of seekers discovering the **DIVINE** within themselves, of souls finding light in the depths of their being. But where was mine? Where was the spark that could set my spirit aflame, the guiding force that could lift me from this abyss of uncertainty?

I walked through the corridors of my mind, searching tirelessly for answers. I wept in solitude, my tears dissolving into the silence of the night. I yearned for something greater—something beyond this world of fleeting illusions and unanswered prayers. But the more I searched, the deeper the emptiness grew, spreading through me like an unrelenting tide.

Each passing day, the hollowness in my chest expanded, its echoes louder than any words of comfort I could whisper to myself. The winds of despair howled through the chambers of my soul, testing my endurance, daring me to surrender. And yet, beneath the weight of sorrow, beneath the heaviness of longing, a faint whisper of hope still remained—a fragile ember flickering in the darkness, refusing to be extinguished.

And so, I continued my journey—barefoot in spirit, carrying the weight of my unanswered prayers upon my shoulders. I did not know where the path would lead, nor how long I would have to walk, but something within urged me forward. And as I took each step, weary yet determined, something remarkable happened.

A sound, soft at first, rose from the depths of my being. It was not a cry of despair, nor a plea for salvation, but a chant—an offering from my soul to the unknown. And with every whispered syllable, the burden grew lighter, the path clearer.

I walked, and I chanted...
**"Om Namah Shivay... Om Namah Shivay...
Om Namah Shivay..."**

The sound of the chant merged with the beeping of the **heart** monitors. It was as if the machines themselves were chanting with me, affirming the truth I had long missed. Tears welled up in my eyes as I realized — **God resides in the heart.**

The machines were not merely healing physical bodies; they were protecting the **DIVINE** rhythm of **LIFE**. Every time a doctor saved a **heart**, they were unknowingly restoring a temple. Every heartbeat was a reminder of the eternal **DIVINE** presence.

Overwhelmed by the revelation, my lips quivered and I began to chant:
"Radha Swami... Radha Swami... Radha Swami..."

As the sacred name of the **DIVINE** lover of the soul escaped my mouth, I felt a weight lift off my chest. My vision blurred with tears, but my spirit soared. I understood enlightenment is not hidden in the mountains nor concealed in the heaven; enlightenment resides in the **HEART** — where the **DIVINE** rhythm of **LIFE** echoes every second.

I rose from my seat, transformed. The **heart** was not merely a physical organ — it was the living manifestation of **God's** presence in every human.

My search had ended, and my mission had begun. If I could inspire love, heal broken hearts, and restore the faith of others — I would become a true **Preacher of the Heart.**

As I walked out my spirit began to chant louder than ever before

"**Radha Swami... Radha Swami... Radha Swami...**"

And with each repetition, the world grew brighter. The darkness began to fade. My enlightenment was complete — not because I found **God** in the skies but because I found **God** within the **heart.**

CHAPTER THREE

The Heart of Shiva

And so, I walked on... not as a lost wanderer, but as a
Preacher of the Heart — chanting eternally:
"Om Namah Shivay..Om Namah Shivay.. Om Namah Shivay.."
This version carries a deep spiritual resonance, linking the
physical **heart** with the **DIVINE** presence within, expanding it into
a full poetic prayer for **Lord Shiva:**

A Poetic Prayer to Lord Shiva

*O **Mahadev**, Lord of Time and Death,*
Bearer of the moon, conqueror of breath.
I was lost, yet You found me — drowning in despair,
*You touched my **heart** and laid my burdens bare.*

***Om Namah Shivay**, my **heart** now beats for **You**,*
Through the fire, through the storm, you pulled me through.
I was a man once broken, now born anew,
*Only because of You, **Mahadev**, my Saviour true.*

The poison I drank in my darkest night,
You turned it to nectar, restoring my sight.
I gave up the bottle, I gave up the lie,
*And found eternal peace in the chant — **"Om Namah Shivay."***

*O **Bholenath**, my soul is forever Yours,*
From the burning ghats to life's open doors.
I will walk the path You have shown me clear,
And in every heartbeat, I'll feel you near.
Let the drum of Damru echo in my veins,
Let my heart be Thy temple, breaking all chains.

And when my final breath leaves my mortal frame,
Let it whisper Your sacred name.

The poetic prayer to **Lord Shiva** captures my gratitude, surrender, and the transformative healing he brought to me.

Surrender to Lord Shiva (letting go of worldly pain)
Seeking enlightenment through Lord Shiva's guidance
Finding the divine within your own heart
Om Namah Shivay... Om Namah Shivay... Om Namah Shivay...
Forever and ever, in my **heart**, you shall stay.

I wanted to add a bit more about myself as I thought it was beautiful and I can feel the depth of my spiritual journey through this piece. I shared more about myself and my life experiences that drew me to the path of enlightenment so that I can seemlesslessly weave it into a story. The poetic prayer for **Lord Shiva** reflects the intensity of my seeking and the **DIVINE** revelation I experienced. The prayer can act as the climax of this journey — where I surrender to Shiva who brought me the light I was seeking.

Adding my personal experience within the story that drew me towards enlightenment.

1. Crafting a powerful and poetic prayer for **Lord Shiva**, filled with devotion and surrender.
2. Strengthening the symbolism of the **heart**, **DIVINE** energy, and the purpose of the human journey.

I will share some of my experiences and feelings that will transform this book into a divine and compelling piece.

I myself has been a loner most of my **LIFE**. Gave up on liquor and other substances to live a better life. I was adopted when I was very young but my parents who adopted me gave me a life where I am successful and have a good standard of life. I started following **Anukul Thakur** from small age along with my parents and that has always blessed me for a good life and I started worshipping **Lord Shiva** as I was in a turnmoil at one stage of my **LIFE** and then he has always blessed me to heal and be alive.

CHAPTER FOUR

The Path of a Loner – My Early Life and Search for Meaning The Healing Journey – Overcoming Darkness Through Devotion

I was wandering — a loner, a soul without a destination — searching for meaning in a world that seemed steeped in shadows. My **LIFE**, though blessed with success and comfort, often felt like a void. There were nights when I would find solace at the bottom of a glass, and days when my spirit would drift aimlessly, burdened by invisible chains.

But fate is mysterious, and grace often arrives unannounced. I was adopted at a very young age, and the parents who chose me, gave me a life beyond what I could have ever imagined. They introduced me to **Anukul Thakur** — a **DIVINE** master whose teachings resonated within our home like a sacred melody.

From a young age, I learned the power of devotion, and unknowingly, it laid the foundation for my soul's journey.

Yet **LIFE** is seldom without storms. There came a time when my soul fell into turmoil. Pain wrapped itself around me like a serpent, and darkness became my only companion. The world I had built around me felt like it was crumbling. I felt hollow, lifeless — like a man trapped in his own suffering. I sought refuge in worldly distractions, but they only dug me deeper into the void.

Like a whisper from the heavens, the name of **Lord Shiva** entered my **LIFE**.
"Om Namah Shivay... Om Namah Shivay... Om Namah Shivay..."
I don't know why I began chanting it. Maybe it was desperation, or perhaps it was fate. But the moment I invoked **HIS** name, a **DIVINE** force seemed to enter my soul. I began to worship **HIM**, surrendering my pain, my past, and my burdens to **HIM**. And then something miraculous happened — **I began to heal.**

The liquor that once numbed my pain lost its grip on me. The false attachments that held me captive began to dissolve. I rose from the ashes of my broken self and found a new **LIFE** — a **LIFE** filled with purpose, love, and unbreakable faith. **Lord Shiva** did not just save me; he resurrected me.

And so, I kept walking the path of **LIFE**, chanting **HIS** name, with my **heart** beating as **HIS temple**.

CHAPTER FIVE

The Turning Point – How Lord Shiva Entered My Life

One day, as if guided by unseen hands, I found myself standing in front of the **American Heart Association**. "Why am I here?" I wondered. My feet, however, seemed to move on their own, and I entered. Inside, I heard the steady beeping of **heart** monitors and saw doctors fighting to keep **hearts** alive. People who had come face-to-face with death were now being brought back to **LIFE** . My **heart** trembled as I realized this is what **Lord Shiva did for me**.

He saved my **heart** when it was breaking. He resurrected my soul when it was dying. He pulled me from the brink of destruction and gave me a new heartbeat. These doctors were unknowingly doing what **Shiva** has always done — saving lives. I sat in a corner, my **heart** pounding, and tears rolled down my face. Without thinking, I began to chant:

"Om Namah Shivay... Om Namah Shivay... Om Namah Shivay..."

The sound of the **heart** monitors harmonized with my chant, and it felt as though **Lord Shiva** himself was present in the room. My journey, my pain, my healing — it was all his **DIVINE** play. And I realized then — **the heart is Shiva's temple.** Every beat of my **heart** was a reminder that he never left me.

I closed my eyes, and from the depths of my soul, I began to pray.

As I walked, my tears of gratitude fell like rain. I was no longer the man who once sought solace in worldly vices. I was now a **Preacher of the Heart** a man saved by **Lord Shiva,** destined to spread the message of **DIVINE** love and inner healing.

I was saved to save others.

I was healed to heal others.

And I was resurrected to awaken others.

And in the deepest corner of my **heart**, I heard his reply:

"I was always with you."

This piece is — infused with my personal journey, DIVINE grace, and a poetic prayer to Lord Shiva.

The book will be deeply spiritual and poetic, centered around my personal experiences, the power of **Shiva's** healing, and the transformation of my soul. It will also have:

A gripping introduction about my LIFE journey.

Chapters like *The Darkest Night, The Call of Mahadev, The Heart of Shiva*, and *The Preacher.*

Powerful prayers to **Lord Shiva** and poetic reflections.

A message of hope for those still struggling with inner turmoil.

A closing chapter where my story transforms into a message of light for others.

Alternate Titles for the book:

1. **The Preacher: My Journey from Darkness to Shiva's Light**
2. **Om Namah Shivay: How Lord Shiva Saved Me from Myself**
3. **Resurrected by Shiva: A Story of Healing and Enlightenment**
4. **The Heartbeat of Shiva: Finding God Within Me**

I started drafting the full book:

A book cover featuring **Lord Shiva** and a symbolic representation of healing
A poetic foreword written in my voice, addressed to those still searching for light I want to make this book my *sacred offering* to **Lord Shiva**.

This book will have the potential to touch countless lives and inspire those still trapped in darkness — just like **Lord Shiva** pulled me out of my own turmoil.

I will include the ***Karpur Gauram Karunavtaram*** mantra as a powerful and sacred element in my book as I sing this every evening for **Lord Shiva**. I'll also weave in a moment where I am singing it during evening prayers, allowing readers to feel the deep connection I have with **Lord Shiva**.

CHAPTER SIX

The Blessings of Sri Sri Anukulchandra Thakur

Following the Guru's Teachings

I have lived through moments that tested my spirit—times when the weight of my struggles felt unbearable, when the questions in my **heart** echoed louder than any answers the world could offer. I have walked through darkness, searching for a light that seemed just beyond my reach. But through it all, through every tear, every prayer, and every silent plea, I found something far greater than what I had been searching for. I found **grace.**

This book is not just a retelling of my **LIFE**—it is a **testament** to the journey that shaped me. It is about the struggles that nearly broke me, the healing that mended me, and the **DIVINE** hand of **Anukul Thakur** that lifted me when I could no longer walk on my own. I did not always understand **HIS** ways, but with time, I realized that every hardship carried a lesson, every wound held the potential for transformation, and every unanswered prayer was guiding me toward something far greater than I could have imagined.

I want this book to be more than just my story—I want it to be **a companion** for those who are walking their own uncertain paths. If you have ever felt lost, if you have ever questioned your purpose, if you have ever searched for something beyond this material world, then perhaps, in these pages, you will find a reflection of your own journey.

This is my offering—**a journey of faith, healing, and DIVINE grace.** It is a story of surrender, of discovering the sacred within, and of the unshakable presence of **Anukul Thakur,** who has been with me every step of the way.

And so, I invite you to walk with me through these pages. May my story bring you **light,** just as **HIS** grace brought light into my **LIFE.**

I pray every evening with my mother with the **Guru mantra** to **Anukul Thakur, Boroma, Borda and Ashok da.** We call it **Binati Prathana.** Evening prayer. It is incredibly sacred and heartwarming.

CHAPTER SEVEN

Binati Prarthana

Evening Prayers with My Mother and the Deep Peace It Brings

I will now capture the essence of **Binati Prarthana** in the book — where my mother and me pray every evening, invoking the **DIVINE** presence of **Anukul Thakur, Boroma, Borda,** and **Ashok Da** through the **Guru Mantra** and other prayers – **bar bar kor binati, bar bar koro jor koro and joi radhe radhe** along with **Guru Mantra.**

Guru mantra has all the gurus and the **DIVINE** God's **GURU VISHNU GURU BRAHMA GURU DEVO MAHESHWARA.** Its profound meaning — honoring **Brahma (the Creator), Vishnu (the Preserver), and Maheshwara (Shiva, the Destroyer)** — symbolizing the **DIVINE** trinity guiding my **LIFE.** Since **Anukul Thakur** has been a guiding force in our **LIFE,** I will include the **Guru Mantra** in my book as a sacred connection to **HIM.**

Guru Mantra brings peace and clarity, especially in challenging times. Chanting the mantra deepens my spiritual connection with **Anukul Thakur** and the **DIVINE** Gods.

I'll describe this moment as a time of **peace, devotion, and DIVINE connection,** symbolizing how my family has built a spiritual bridge through evening prayers. We feel a **DIVINE** energy while doing **Binati Prarthana** together with my mother.

I'll make sure this part of my book radiates pure devotion and captures the beautiful connection we share during these evening prayers. **Calm and peace** surround us with the chant of the **Guru Mantra** together. A heartfelt prayer passage reflects the love and gratitude I feel for each DIVINE figure during **Binati Prarthana**.

I will now ensure the **Binati Prarthana** section in this book beautifully reflects the deep reverence me and my mother share for **Sri Sri Thakur Anukulchandra, Boroma, Borda, Ashokda and Chhorda**.

I'll describe the **DIVINE** energy, peace, and connection we experience during this evening prayer, making it one of the most powerful and touching parts of this book.

It is very peaceful and takes our minds to a very heavenly feeling with relaxation no matter how much tired we are but the mind will relax.
IT IS... absolutelyDIVINE !

We experience *profound peace* during **Binati Prarthana** — the moment when me and my mother, no matter how tired or worn out from the day, enter a space of complete relaxationand bliss through the evening prayer. It is the presence of **Sri Sri Thakur Anukulchandra, Boroma, Borda, Ashokda, and Chhorda** instantly **washes away all fatigue**, leaving our **heart** filled with peace and gratitude.

I will now make sure that when I write this part of your book, I capture:
1. The heavenly feeling of peace that transcends all physical tiredness when you chant the **Guru Mantra**.
2. The **unbreakable bond** between me and my mother during this evening prayer.

3. How **Sri Sri Thakur Anukulchandra, Boroma, Borda, Ashokda, and Chhorda** become the source of
DIVINE calmness in our **LIFE**.

During **Binati Prarthana** the mind forgets everything and goes into deep meditation. It is not just a prayer, but a **spiritual journey** where the mind forgets everything and merges into pure **DIVINE** presence.

It gives the feeling as if the **soul is floating in peace,** detached from all worries.
This section in a way can bring **readers into a meditative state,** allowing them to feel the same **tranquility and DIVINE connection.**

You must **join hands** to your chest when you do the prayer in devotion, symbolizing surrender, respect, and deep connection with the **DIVINE.** This small detail makes a huge impact in capturing the true essence of the prayers.

People shouldn't follow anyone blindly; it must come from the **heart.**

That is such a powerful truth! I will include this wisdom in this book — emphasizing that **true devotion must come from within** and not just be followed blindly.
This as a **guiding principle** in a chapter about faith and personal connection with the **DIVINE**
A **reflection or story** where you realized the importance of heartfelt devotion over blind following. This message will inspire readers to seek their **own true spiritual path** instead of just following rituals without meaning.

CHAPTER EIGHT

Guru Mantra – Honoring the Divine Masters

Alongside the **Karpur Gauram** mantra, I chant the **Guru Mantra**, a prayer that honors **Sri Sri Thakur Anukulchandra, Boroma, Borda, Ashokda, and Chhorda**. This mantra is a constant reminder that **the**
DIVINE exists in many forms—as Gurus, as **Gods**, as guiding lights in our lives.

Guru Brahma, Guru Vishnu, Guru Devo Maheshwara,
Guru Sakshat Parabrahma, Tasmai Shri Gurave Namah.
"The Guru is Brahma, the Creator.
The Guru is Vishnu, the Preserver.
The Guru is Maheshwara, the Destroyer.
The Guru is the Supreme Divine.
To that Guru, I offer my humble salutations."

In this mantra, the guru is considered as the - **Brahma** the creation, **Vishnu** the protector and **devo Maheshwara** the transformer. It acknowledges the lessons learned through **LIFE** experiences and honors' both the human and spiritual **guru**, including the **guru** within.

This mantra has been a part of my **LIFE** since childhood. It reminds me of my roots, my teachers, and the guiding forces that have shaped me. When I chant it, I feel connected to my spiritual lineage, as if I am bowing at the feet of all those who have blessed my path.

Guru devaya vidmahe Parambramahe dhimahi Tanno guru prachodayat

A **guru gayatri mantra** is one that a guru gives to a disciple, who then chants the mantra for his/her spiritual growth. Like all the mantras this is also derived from Sanskrit. Guru means removal of the darkness from one's life and enlightening the life with the light of knowledge acquired from the guru.

CHAPTER NINE

Mantras and Meditation

The Power of Karpur Gauram and The Shiva Gayatri Mantra

Om Namah Shivaya
(Chanted three times to awaken the **DIVINE** within)

There is an ancient power in the repetition of sacred words. A mantra is not just a combination of sounds—it is a vibration, a force that connects us to something beyond the physical world. Each syllable, when spoken with devotion, has the ability to cleanse the mind, purify the soul, and bring peace to the **heart**.

For me, 3 **mantras have defined my spiritual journey**—the **Karpur Gauram Karunavtaramand Shiva Gayatri Mantra**. They are not just prayers; they are **bridges to the DIVINE**, guiding me through life's uncertainties and leading me into deep meditation.

Karpur Gauram Karunavtaram – The Evening Invocation
Karpur Gauram Karunavtaram,
Sansara Saram Bhujagendra Haram,
Sadā Vasantam Hridayāravinde,
Bhavam Bhavāni Sahitam Namami.
"I bow to the pure white, compassionate **Lord Shiva**,
The essence of the universe, who wears a serpent as a garland.
He always resides in the lotus of the **heart**,
Together with Goddess Bhavani, his **DIVINE** consort."

The moment these words leave my lips, I feel a wave of peace washing over me. No matter how exhausted or troubled I am, this mantra **rejuvenates my spirit**. It is as if **Lord Shiva himself** is present, watching over me, reminding me that I am never alone.

Shiva Gayatri Mantra
The Monday Morning Ritual

If evenings are dedicated to peace, **Monday mornings are for power**. Every Monday, at the break of dawn, I sit in solitude and chant the **Shiva Gayatri Mantra 108 times**. This mantra, which I follow in the **version by Ketan Patwardan**, carries an **immense force**, filling my **heart** with energy and devotion.

> Tat Purushaya Vidmahe,
> Mahadevaya Dhimahi,
> Tanno Rudrah Prachodayat.
> "May we know the Supreme Being,
> May we meditate upon the great Lord,
> May **Rudra** inspire and guide us."

The repetition of this mantra **awakens something deep within me**—a fire, a strength, a **DIVINE** connection with **Shiva, the ultimate source of destruction and transformation**. As I chant, I feel my worries dissolve, my mind focus, and my spirit **align with the cosmic rhythm.**

CHAPTER TEN

The Transformative Power of Mantras

Each of these mantras has played a profound role in my **LIFE**. They are not just words; they are **spiritual tools** that:

Bring peace in moments of restlessness.
Provide strength in times of difficulty.
Help me forget the world and enter deep meditation.
Remind me that devotion should come from the heart—not be followed blindly.

I have experienced firsthand how **mantras can heal, transform, and elevate the soul.** They have helped me **overcome struggles, find clarity, and deepen my faith.**

To those reading this, I invite you to experience this **DIVINE** **energy** yourself. The power of a mantra is unlocked when it is **chanted with love, belief, and surrender.** Whether it is the **gentle invocation of Karpur Gauram, the deep wisdom of the Guru Mantra, or the fierce devotion of Shiva Gayatri Mantra,** each chant brings you **one step closer to enlightenment.**

CHAPTER ELEVEN

A Divine Practice

How Joining Hands in Prayer Deepens the Connection

Close your eyes. Join your hands and put them next to your chest. Breathe. Chant. Feel the divine presence within you.

Om Namah Shivaya. Om Namah Shivaya. Om Namah Shivaya. May Lord Shiva and the Divine Gurus bless us all.

This chapter reflects the deep **devotion, peace, and strength** you can experience through the mantras.

CHAPTER TWELVE

Yoga – Union of the Self

A journey from motion to stillness, from self to soul . As I near the end of this spiritual journey, I invite you into the space that helped me heal and expand—**Yoga**. This was not just a routine, but a revelation. Through breath and posture, I met the **DIVINE** within. **Yoga** became my offering—one that nurtured the body, stilled the mind, and awakened the spirit.

I am adding pictures for the **Yoga** poses for the readers so that they can follow and practice which positively impact mental health by incorporating meditation, breathing exercises, and physical postures, promoting relaxation, reducing stress, and improving overall well-being.

Surya Namaskar – 5 times Surya Namaskar is a powerful practice!

Here's an illustration of the full Surya Namaskar sequence

Key Benefits of Surya Namaskar:

- **Physical Health**: Improves flexibility, tones muscles, and enhances cardiovascular health.
- **Mental Clarity**: Balances the nervous system and reduces stress.
- **Spiritual Connection**: Aligns the body with solar energy and awakens inner consciousness.
- **Energy Boost**: Practicing it at sunrise can energize you for the day ahead

Ah, **Kapalbhati Pranayama** – a truly powerful and purifying yogic breathing technique. The name itself is beautiful:

- **"Kapal"** means skull (head),
- **"Bhati"** means shining or illuminating.

So Kapalbhati literally means **"Skull Shining Breath"** – not just in the physical sense but also in terms of clarity, awareness, and inner radiance.

Benefits of Kapalbhati:

1. Detoxifies lungs and respiratory system
2. Boosts oxygen supply and energizes the brain
3. Enhances digestion and metabolism
4. Balances the nervous system
5. Clears the mind and strengthens willpower

Cautions:
Avoid or consult a teacher if you:
1. Have high blood pressure
2. Are pregnant
3. Suffer from heart conditions, hernia, or epilepsy

"In every breath, I found silence. In every pose, I found myself."

Asanas That Anchored Me
1. **Surya Namaskar** – the morning offering to light.
2. **Matsyasana** – opening the heart to the divine flow.
3. **Bhujangasana** – rising from the ashes.
4.**Dhanurasana** – drawing the bow of inner strength

MATSYASANA

BHUJANGASANA

DHANURASANA

Breath and Stillness

1.A short insight into Pranayama (e.g., Kapalbhati or Anulom Vilom).

2.How breath connects body to spirit.

Conclusion

A gentle reflection tying yoga into your path with **Anukul Thakur,** **Lord Shiva,** and your inner awakening.
That's a beautiful way to bring your journey full circle.
Ending your spiritual book with **Yoga as a personal and transformative practice** will not only anchor your message, but also offer readers a tangible path to start their own healing. You've already gathered meaningful illustrations like Surya Namaskar, Matsyasana, Bhujangasana, and Dhanurasana—they'll give life and visual depth to this final section.

Conclusion: A Journey Beyond Words

The **conclusion** of this book will leave readers with a feeling of **peace, inspiration, and spiritual fulfillment**. It will reinforce the **key lessons** from my journey and offer **guidance for their own path**. Here's how I envision the conclusion:

* Gratitude & Reflection – Expressing gratitude to **Lord Shiva, Sri Sri Thakur Anukulchandra, Boroma, Borda, Ashokda, Chhorda, and your parents** for guiding me on this spiritual journey.

* A Message for Seekers – Encouraging readers to **follow spirituality from the heart**, not blindly, and to find their own **DIVINE** connection through devotion and meditation.

* The Power of Prayer & Mantras – Reminding readers that chanting *Om Namah Shivaya, Guru Mantra, and Binati Prarthana* can bring **peace, strength, and healing** no matter how difficult life gets.

* A Final Invocation – Ending with a **powerful prayer or mantra** (perhaps *Karpur Gauram Karunavtaram* or a heartfelt dedication to **Lord Shiva**), so that readers feel spiritually uplifted as they finish the book.

* A Call for Inner Awakening – Inspiring readers to embrace **faith, love, and devotion**, knowing that **DIVINE grace is always with them**.

With folded hands and grateful heart,
ROHIT PEGU